Stories
from
Native North America

by
Linda Raczek

Illustrated by
Richard Hook

WAYLAND

OTHER MULTICULTURAL STORIES:

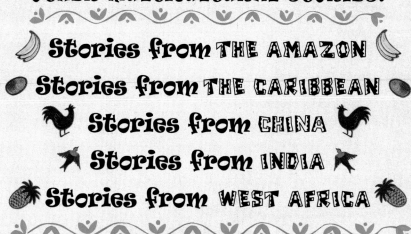

Stories from THE AMAZON

Stories from THE CARIBBEAN

Stories from CHINA

Stories from INDIA

Stories from WEST AFRICA

Series Editor: Paul Mason
Art Director: Jane Hawkins
Designer: Tessa Barwick
Production Controller: Carol Titchener
Printer/binder: G. Canale & C.S.p.A., Turin, Italy

This edition published in 2000 by
Wayland Publishers Ltd
61 Western Rd, Hove
East Sussex, BN3 1JD, England

www.wayland.co.uk

British Library Cataloguing in Publication Data
Raczek, Linda
Stories from Native North America – Folklore – Juvenile literature
2. Tales – United States – Juvenile literature
I. Title II. Hook, Richard
398.2'0973

ISBN 0 7502 2433 9

Contents

Introduction

Native North America. For me, these three words are a window to the past, as well as part of the present. There were once hundreds of tribes and bands living freely in North America. All were unique, rich in their own cultures, languages, appearance - and yes, stories.

Sadly, many tribes have not survived to modern life. But all across Canada and the USA there are still islands of Native North America, where the cultures of America's first peoples continue.

One of these islands, the Ute Mountain Ute Reservation, is where I became the mother of two adopted Native American children, a boy and a girl. Their tribes, and many others, continue to pass on the wisdom, humour and sense of the supernatural that are the trademarks of Native American stories.

Lynda

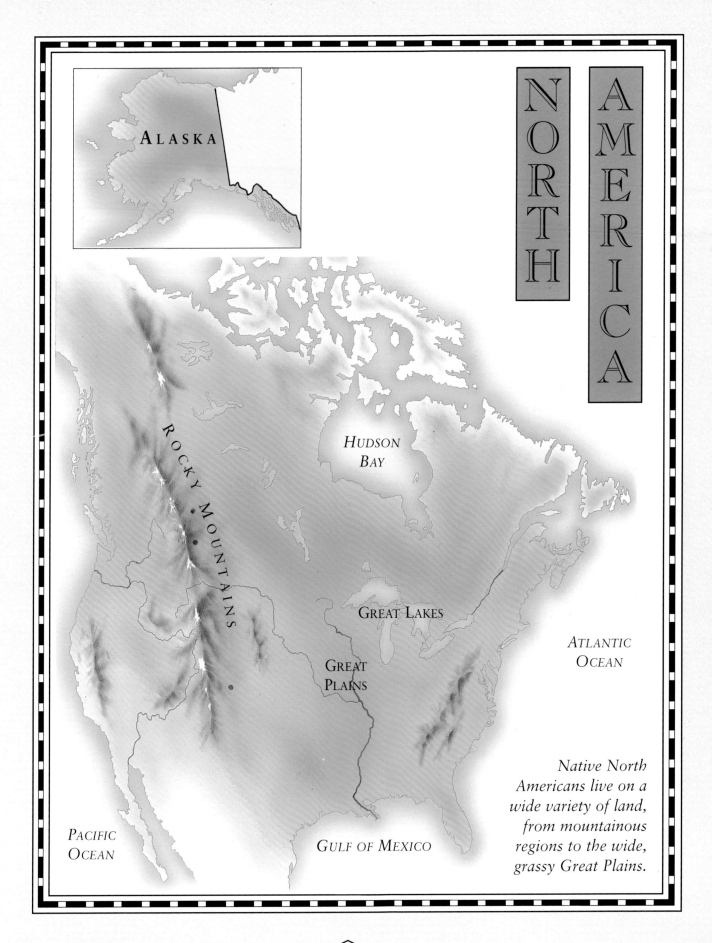

ALASKA

NORTH AMERICA

ROCKY MOUNTAINS

HUDSON BAY

GREAT LAKES

GREAT PLAINS

ATLANTIC OCEAN

PACIFIC OCEAN

GULF OF MEXICO

Native North Americans live on a wide variety of land, from mountainous regions to the wide, grassy Great Plains.

DESERT GHOSTS

Some of the largest Indian reservations stretch across the American Southwest. If you believe the stories from this region, the stark deserts are haunted by witches, skin walkers, water babies and spirits. And when you drive across them at night you begin to wonder – did I just see one?

This story took place only a few years ago in my daughter Autumn's homeland. As you read it, picture the place where the story happened. To the west you can see a black hulk of a mountain, the Sleeping Ute, which looks like a man lying on his back. To the east, the moon rises over the barren ridge of world-famous Mesa Verde National Park. Thousands of mysterious cliff dwellings tell of an ancient people who once lived there and now have vanished.

Listen in as Autumn's grandfather tells a ghost story set in that spine-chilling setting.

Mesa Verde National Park contains hundreds of Indian village ruins up to 1,300 years old.

Ghost of the Ancient One

(A True Story)

When I was a young man, I wanted to be a tribal policeman. They rode around the reservation in their shiny new cars, helping people and locking up the ones in trouble. But all those jobs went to the goody-two-shoes, not guys like me who were a little bit wild. Then one night I had my chance.

It was the blackest of nights, and the moon was only a sliver coming up over Mesa Verde. I looked out of my window into the darkness and heard an owl hooting in the distance. I always thought of myself as a modern Indian. I didn't believe in the old superstitions. Still, the eerie sound of the owl's call made me shiver. In the Ute way, the owl always warns of death.

Then the phone rang loudly and I almost jumped. It was the chief of tribal police.

'Miikwa,' I greeted him. 'What's the trouble?'

I heard him sigh. 'Raymond, we need a night-watchman up at the gravel pit. There's been some kids causing trouble up there, starting fires and the like.' He hesitated. 'The other officers don't want to go. Are you interested?'

I knew why no one wanted the job. Everyone believed the gravel pit was haunted. People claimed they heard the chanting of the Ancient Ones, the ancestors who once lived in cliff dwellings on Mesa Verde. Sometimes people said they saw the glowing spirits of the Ancient Ones streaming down the face of the mesa and into the black, gaping hole of the gravel pit.

But, like I said, I didn't believe in those old superstitions. And here was my chance to become a policeman.

The road to the gravel pit was lonely and dark. It led me away from the comforting lights of the houses, toward the darkness of the gravel pit. When I parked at the edge, it was hard to tell where the black hole ended and the sky began.

Time passed slowly alone in the car, but I admit I was too nervous to walk around. The place was deathly quiet. I thought of the owl and wondered if the warning had been for me.

Suddenly a light flickered across the pit. Soon another light, then another glowed. Was it the Ancient Ones? A chill shuddered through me, but I quickly shook it off. Surely it was just some teenagers starting brush fires, just as the chief had said.

But through the open window came the faint
sound of chanting. The eerie warbling sent a shiver up
my spine. I quickly rolled up my window and locked the
doors. I closed my eyes and tried to shut out the sights
and sounds of the ancient ones making their nightly trek
into the haunted cavern.

I must have fallen asleep, for when I opened my eyes
again, the thin moon was high overhead. Something had
jarred me awake. Sitting in the darkness, I was astonished
to feel the whole car shake. It was as if large men were
rocking the car on its springs.

My first thought was to turn on the headlights. Nothing moved in the twin pools of yellow light. I started the car and drove around in a tight circle. Nothing. By now I was thinking I had imagined it all. The car shook violently again and I slammed on the gas, tyres screeching and throwing gravel as I sped away.

I could feel something behind me! The little hairs on the back of my neck stood on end as I tried to outrun that terrifying presence. Once more, the car shook and almost bounced off the road. But the thought of reaching home, the friendly lights of my neighbours and the safety of my familiar life kept me going until I outran the ghost.

That night I turned to my grandfather for help in the old ways. Blinking away sleep, he made a small fire. When it had burned down to glowing coals, he spoke.

'Grandson, sit here. The sacred cedar will clean away any evil from touching death and the spirit world.'

He sprinkled cedar on the coals and swirled the smoke over me with a fan of eagle feathers.

'Raymond, cedar woman tells me you must return to the haunted place. One of the old ones needs your help.'

Who was I to question the ways of our tribe? If I was to become a tribal policeman, I had to put away my fears.

At dawn I drove back to the gravel pit. As sunlight splintered over the jagged mesa, I stood over the skeleton of one of my elders. I knew from the tattered clothes nearby that these were the remains of the blind grandfather we called Old Man Coyote. He had wandered away years ago and had been missing ever since. His family's grief time had never ended. I knew now we could send this Ancient One on his way with our blessings, in the Ute way. Only then would the hauntings end.

And that, my young friends, is how I became a tribal policeman.

TWO TRICKSTER TALES

The most popular figure in Native American stories is the Trickster. Sometimes he is a coyote, but other animals, like beavers, crows and racoons, are also likely Tricksters. Human-like characters with fun names such as Manabozho, Nanabusho, and Kuloscap are great favourites of Native American children.

Funny or serious, Trickster stories always teach a lesson. And even though Trickster is greedy, lazy, and a fool whose clever ideas backfire again and again – there's a little bit of Trickster in all of us.

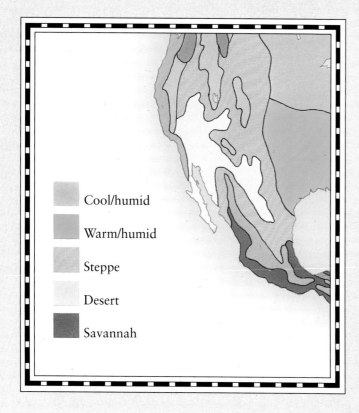

Cool/humid

Warm/humid

Steppe

Desert

Savannah

Coyotes originally roamed over the southwest deserts of the USA. Now they can be found all over the USA.

Coyote and Old Turkey

(San Juan Pueblo)

Everybody knows Coyote is very lazy. One day Coyote surprised his wife by saying, 'I think I'll go hunting.'

But Coyote only chose that day to go hunting because it had snowed a little during the night. That, he thought, would make it very easy to track something to eat.

Sure enough, just a little ways up the hill, Coyote saw some tracks. He followed them and found Old Turkey up on the mesa. Everybody knows turkeys aren't very smart.

'Old Turkey,' he said. 'Go tell my wife to make some turkey stew for me.'

'But how will I ever find your house?' Old Turkey asked dumbly.

'Just follow my tracks in the snow,' said Coyote.

After Old Turkey left,
Coyote chuckled at his good
fortune. Here it was early in the
day and his supper was as good as
done. It was warm on top of the mesa, so he
laid down and took a nap.

When Old Turkey came to Coyote's house, he saw
Coyote's wife sewing moccasins with strings of sinew drying
over the fireplace.

'Granddaughter,' he said, 'your husband sent me to tell
you to cook up some of that sinew for supper.'

That didn't make sense to Mrs Coyote, but Old Turkey
was her elder so she did as he said.

Coyote woke up dreaming of delicious turkey stew.
When he got home, he was really hungry. His wife put out
a bowl of stew for him.

'This turkey is as tough as sinew!' he grumbled.

With that, Coyote's wife knew her husband had once
again been up to his old tricks. 'Why, Old Turkey said you
wanted that sinew cooked up for dinner,' she said.

Then Coyote knew he had been outsmarted by Old
Turkey.

Manabozho and the Elk Skull

(Ojibwa)

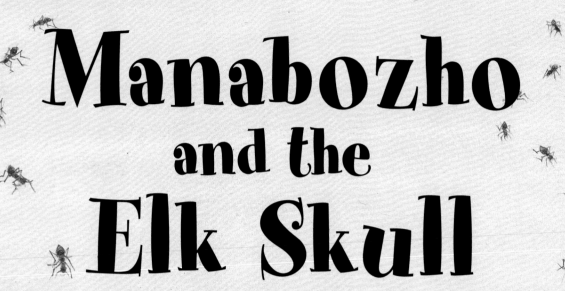

Manabozho was out walking in the woods. He was hungry. When he came upon an old elk skull, he watched the ants crawling in and out of it.

'I wish I was a little ant so I could do that. Then I could find something to eat!'

His magic turned him instantly into an ant, and he crawled into the old skull.

But Manabozho's luck changed and the spell wore off. While he was inside the skull, he suddenly turned back into himself. His head was stuck inside the skull!

Well, Manabozho went stumbling through the forest, yelling for help. He couldn't see and kept bumping into trees. The people in the village saw him coming and said: 'It's the Elk Spirit. He is angry and crazy. Give him whatever he wants!'

Manabozho let them think he was a spirit. Otherwise they might just laugh at him and leave him stuck in the skull.

'A long life to you! Bring me food!' he shouted. Then he slipped and fell on a rock, hitting his head. The elk skull broke off.

'It's just Manabozho!' the people cried, as he ran back into the woods.

NATIVES OF THE NORTH

Imagine the cold, dark winters of northern Canada and Alaska. Now imagine surviving such a winter with nothing but handmade tools, your skill at hunting or fishing, and the people of your tribe to rely on.

In the harsh Arctic lands, a lazy or careless man can easily meet with misfortune. Not only that – he can bring misfortune upon his family and friends as well. In this tale, the villagers have been patient. But what are they to do with Qasi, now that he had gone too far?

The two main Native American tribes in Alaska are the Inuit (Eskimo) and Aleuts.

Qasi, the Great Liar
(Inuit)

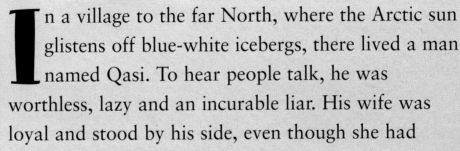

In a village to the far North, where the Arctic sun glistens off blue-white icebergs, there lived a man named Qasi. To hear people talk, he was worthless, lazy and an incurable liar. His wife was loyal and stood by his side, even though she had grown tired of the scorn and ridicule of the village people. Qasi and his wife had no children.

They lived together in a shack, with only the poorest furnishings, and clothing made of raven's skins.

Now it was Qasi's weakness to take a shortcut in everything that involved work. When the men went out hunting, Qasi never came home with anything. So for years he provided for his wife by trickery and deceit – anything to get out of honest work.

Each day he paddled out to sea in his kayak with the other hunters. But soon he was complaining bitterly to himself: 'I have such terrible luck. Why should I even try to hunt?'

One time he watched as another hunter dragged a very large seal up onto the shore of an island. When this man headed back out to sea to continue hunting, sly Qasi towed the seal home to his wife.

'Qasi has killed the biggest seal of the day!' she boasted.

But some of the village people noticed that Qasi had pulled the carcass in with a new towline. Shiny bits of narwhal tusk were braided into it.

'Where did you get that beautiful new towline, Qasi?' one asked suspiciously.

'I have always had it,' Qasi lied.

Finally, as the sun set, the last hunter returned.

'Qasi's luck has turned. He has brought home the biggest seal of the day,' the other men told him.

'That's interesting,' the last hunter said. 'Because I myself killed a large seal this morning, but it is gone.'

He marched over to Qasi's shack in the dark and called out politely: 'Qasi, I would like my new towline back.'

Qasi didn't even apologize. He threw out the line and went back to bed. The next day, he acted as though nothing had happened.

Paddling out to sea again, Qasi had another idea. 'I have the worst luck in the world,' he griped. 'If I lost all my hunting gear, I wouldn't have to hunt for a while.'

He tied a large rock to his harpoon line and floats made of seal skin. He threw the rock – splash! – over the side of his kayak. Everything was pulled under water.

Qasi yelled to the hunters in kayaks nearby. 'A great walrus has run off with everything,' he lied. 'If you come upon a large walrus, bring it to me – it's mine!'

But later that day, one of the other hunters found Qasi's harpoon line and floats washed ashore. He returned them to Qasi, saying, 'Here is your fishing gear, Qasi. Here you can see where the rock slipped out.'

Once again, no apology. Qasi acted as if he had done nothing wrong.

On another day, Qasi complained: 'Why hunt? Each time my luck goes from bad to worse.' Then he paddled away from the other men, behind a nearby island. He pulled his kayak ashore and set to work.

First he took his heavy harpoon and beat it against the kayak until the wood splintered, then he took off his clothes and did the same. When he dressed, his raven-skin shirt and breeches were torn and shredded.

At last he lifted up a boulder and dropped it – first on his right foot, then his left. Qasi bit his lip to keep from howling in pain. After a while, he limped back to his kayak.

He filled it with ice and snow, stuffing some into his shirt as well.

When Qasi returned home, everyone felt sorry for him. 'What happened?' they asked.

Qasi winced in real pain. 'An iceberg calved on me while I hunted.' As an added touch, he plucked the tender hair at the back of his neck until a fat tear rolled down his cheek.

Poor Qasi! His feet had to be splinted and wrapped. He had to stay in bed until they healed. Of course, Qasi was quite content to be waited on by his wife and the other villagers. They brought him food each day.

But the day came when some women from the nearby island arrived to visit. 'Where is that crazy man who was dropping rocks on his feet and beating up his kayak? Does he live here?' they asked.

The people were furious. 'We will never believe anything you say, Qasi!' His wife wept with shame, but Qasi didn't even apologize. He acted as though he had done nothing wrong.

'Qasi has gone too far,' some of the men muttered.

'Yes, when winter comes, times will be harder. We can no longer support him and his lying ways.'

'This is your last chance,' they told Qasi.

It was late summer and Qasi was hungry.

He told the other hunters: 'I saw a dead whale washed up on the other side of the island.'

The men grumbled, but they headed out to look for the whale. They made Qasi go with them.

'Where is it?' they asked, when it was nowhere to be seen.

'I think it must be on the next island,' Qasi lied.

When the whale was not there either, Qasi said, 'I must have forgotten where I saw it. Maybe...'

One of the other men joined in. 'Yes, yes, I saw it, too. Let's go to the outermost island.' Everyone, especially Qasi, looked surprised. But they followed.

Out on this forlorn island, with the cold gray ocean pounding its rocky edge, they dragged Qasi ashore. There they stripped him of everything except his underclothes. His skinny pale legs shivered and rippled with goosebumps.

'No! No, don't leave me! I won't lie again,' Qasi pleaded. 'I'm sorry!'

But it was too late. The men looked away as they boarded their kayaks. Only one felt pity – more for Qasi's wife than the Great Liar himself. He threw Qasi an old, rusty knife.

'Prove yourself, Qasi,' the man said. 'You have taken from our hands all these years. Now you must survive with your hands alone. Maybe we will see you again in the spring.'

Then they left him, all alone on the island. They paddled away toward home, just as the sun sank and great hoards of mosquitoes descended on Qasi like flies to a rotting whale.

THE NAVAJO

'Yá'át'eeh!' That's the friendly greeting you would hear visiting the vast, southwestern homeland of the Navajo. Named by the Spanish, the Navajo actually call themselves 'the Diné', or 'the People'.

The Diné became famous during World War II, when their complex language was used as an unbreakable code. But they are also known for their weavings, jewellery and detailed sandpaintings.

When you read the Navajo story of how the world began, you will get an idea of what is important to this tribe of Native Americans.

The sacred mountains in the story are real: Mount Blanca in the east, Mount Taylor in the south, the San Francisco Peaks in the west, and Mount Hesperus in the North. I live near Mount Hesperus, but I have travelled to each of the sacred mountains of the Navajo.

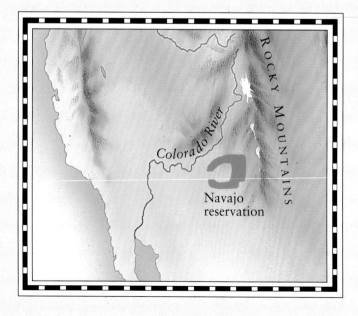

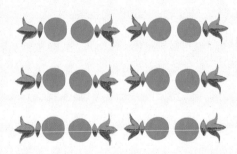

The Navajo is the largest Native American tribe in the USA. Their main reservation covers 62,000 square km.

Navajo Creation Story

I

The world was not always as it is now. Long, long ago, the People say, they lived in a place of darkness. It was called First World. First World was very small, like an island surrounded by mist. In it lived First Man, First Woman, and Coyote, dressed in his long fur robe. Some say there were beings that looked like insects. There was one tree in the centre of the world.

First World became crowded and miserable. The beings argued and fought. Finally, First Man gathered up handfuls of soil from the four directions. He took seeds from the tree so the People would always have firewood. Then he led them to the next world.

II

When First Man poked his head into Second World, he saw that it was blue. Many of the blue creatures were there. The sky was full of blue-coloured birds.

In Second World, things started out good. First Man and First Woman went about making four little mounds in the four directions. They planted trees. But the People became selfish and took what was not theirs. The Swallow People had to order them to leave.

III

Third World had four mountains in the distance, one in each direction, and there was a mighty river down the middle of it. It was a good place.

But it was here that the People had their worst argument. The women and the men became jealous of each other. Mean things were said on both sides.

'We don't even need you,' First Woman said. First Man was so hurt, he gathered up all the men and crossed over to the other side of the river on a raft.

At first the women and men did not miss each other. The women's gardens produced lots of corn, and the men had plenty of meat. But later they looked longingly across the river at each other. One woman even tried to cross the river, but she disappeared into the waves.

After four years, the men and women realized they could not live without each other. The men helped their wives through the strong current to their camp on the other side.

But Coyote would not let the matter end so easily. He went looking for the missing woman who had tried to cross over. Coyote suspected Water Monster had taken her to his house under the rough water. Coyote dove in and, just as he thought, found the missing woman. As he rescued her, he decided to secretly steal one of Water Monster's babies, hiding it under his fur robe.

The next day the People woke to a terrifying sight. A wall of white water rushed toward them from every direction!

First Man had to think quickly to save the People from drowning. He led them to the top of the tallest mountain, the one in the East, but the water kept rising. Then he planted a giant hollow reed, and it grew swiftly toward the sky. The People all climbed through a hole in the sky, but the water still rose, trying to overtake them in the next world! Coyote felt guilty. 'This is why Water Monster is angry with us,' he said. He opened up his robe and dropped the water baby through the hole. The flood waters dried up.

IV

They were in Fourth World, the world of today. First Man and First Woman went about rebuilding the four sacred mountains. They put the sun and the moon in the sky to give light.

In Fourth World, Coyote made up for his mistake. He taught the People about Death. To die means there will always be room in the world for new children.

The People know that there are no new worlds to escape to, for the Fifth and final world is the land of the spirit. So human beings must always work hard to keep from fighting, taking what is not theirs, and becoming selfish or jealous. They must treat all with respect.

In the Fourth World, the People try to live in harmony.

THE HORSE PEOPLE

Horses completely changed the world of the Native American. Can you imagine what life must have been like before the Spanish brought the first horses to North America? The plains peoples followed the great herds of buffalo on foot, with only dogs to carry or pull their belongings from place to place. The horse must have seemed a gift from the Great Spirit. In fact, many stories from that time call them Magic or Sacred Dogs.

The Comanches, Sioux and other tribes have passed down stories of how they came to have horses. Later, the skill of raiding enemy tribes for horses was highly respected, and learning it was a big step in a boy's life. The Sioux medicine man, Black Elk, told this tale about just such a boy.

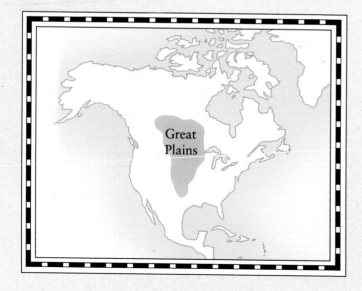

Great
Plains

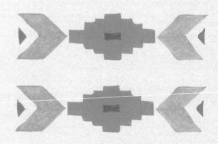

The Great Plains are huge, level grasslands that extend from Texas, in the south, up to Canada.

High Horse's Raid

There was a boy named High Horse who had a great love for a certain girl. He thought she was the most beautiful girl in the world. He couldn't stop thinking about her.

High Horse would wander through their village in a daze, bumping into people, not even smelling the food cooking over the smoky fires. He watched only for the girl. He wanted to speak to her and find out if she liked him, too. But her parents kept her away from boys. High Horse waited for his chance.

Finally, one day at the river, he yelled out to her: 'Do you like me?'

She smiled shyly. 'Yes, a little.'

That was all the encouragement High Horse needed. He took two ponies, which were all that he owned, and went to see the girl's father. He asked to marry her in return for the ponies. The girl's father wouldn't even speak to him.

So High Horse borrowed his cousin Red Deer's two ponies. He offered four ponies for the beautiful girl. But the girl's father continued to ignore him.

High Horse was filled with despair. He had offered all he owned and more for this beautiful girl. What else could be done?

As the days and nights passed, High Horse began to feel crazy with love for this girl. He thought he would die if he could not marry her. Red Deer listened and felt sorry for his friend. 'Cousin, I have an idea, but it takes great courage. Are you willing to do anything?'

'Anything!' High Horse exclaimed, a spark of hope in his eyes.

That night, High Horse and Red Deer met in the moonlight, long after their families were asleep. They blackened their skin with the ashes from a campfire. Quietly, leading their fastest pony, they made their way to the girl's tipi.

'I wish you well, cousin,' Red Deer whispered, as High Horse crawled under the wall of the tipi.

Inside, his eyes slowly became accustomed to the darkness. There, breathing softly, lay his beloved. She was even more beautiful than he remembered. High Horse reached out to touch her and found she was tethered to the ground!

Just then, the girl's father stirred and coughed. High Horse froze. Then he lay down beside the girl to wait until the father was fast asleep.

When High Horse opened his eyes, it was dawn. There he was, lying beside the beautiful girl, only at arm's length away from her parents! High Horse jumped to his feet. He quickly cut the leather thongs holding the girl down and tried to carry her from the tipi. The girl was screaming. The parents were screaming. When High Horse saw that Red Deer and the pony were gone, he started screaming. He dropped the girl and took off running, with many of the village people close at his heels.

High Horse hid out that day, filled with shame. By now he was sick with love. He could not think straight and decided to leave the village forever. But Red Deer had another plan.

'We will go on the war-path together. Are you man enough?'

So the two boys went off together, leaving their village behind. Days later they came upon an enemy camp. In the dark, they silently rounded up all the enemy horses grazing at the edge of camp. Then they ran for their lives, herding the horses ahead of them for three days and nights.

When they reached their village, High Horse and Red Deer drove a hundred horses up to the girl's tipi. This time her father said yes, for he only wanted his daughter to have a good and brave husband. High Horse had proven himself.

STORIES ABOUT NATURE

Native Americans were people of nature. So in the winter – the season that most tribes set aside as the time for telling stories – it makes sense that their stories would be about nature, too.

It is amazing how many tribes believed that in the long ago times, animals and humans could speak to each other. In colourful stories, humans married whales, buffalo, horses, everything under (and including!) the sun. These stories taught respect for other creatures – after all, they were all relatives by marriage!

As Chief Seattle stated: 'If all the beasts were gone, men would die from great loneliness of spirit, for whatever happens to the beasts also happens to man.'

There are 20,000 loons in the Upper Great Lakes in the USA. This represents three-quarters of the loon population outside Alaska, their main homeland.

How Loon outsmarted Winter
(Chippewa, Seneca, Iroquois)

Every year, at the end of summer, Old Man Winter begins his cruel march from the far North. With each step he takes, the ground turns hard and frozen. Each breath brings flurries of snow and icy wind. And fleeing before the Old Man are birds of every kind, heading south to warmer places.

A beautiful loon bobbed on the pond and shivered as Winter arrived. Leaves withered and blew from the trees at the edge of the water. The other birds had already left for their winter homes. But Loon had a tender heart. Her friend Mallard had a broken wing, and was huddled, afraid, in the cattails. Loon did not want to abandon her to Old Man Winter's harsh ways.

Now, loons are known for their crazy laughter during summer nights. But in winter they have no voice. Sadly, once Old Man Winter set up camp nearby, Loon could not even call for help.

When the pond began to freeze over, Loon paddled furiously around in a circle to keep a hole open. Poor Mallard whimpered with hunger. Puffing her sleek feathers out, Loon dove through the hole in the ice. She came up with a nice fat fish for the wounded duck.

Old Man Winter was angry. When Loon dove under again, Old Man blew his breath over the pond and froze the opening closed. Loon was trapped underwater!

But Loon was a quick thinker. She swam underwater to the edge of the pond. There she pulled at a cattail, yanking it down through the ice. She peered up through the little hole left in the ice and pecked until it was big enough for her to get out. Then she and Mallard went to their small wigwam and huddled together for warmth through the night.

But Old Man Winter was not through with them. The next day he peeked in the door of the wigwam. His cold presence alone made icicles form on the walls. Loon and Mallard couldn't help but shiver. Then Loon calmly stirred their small fire and pretended to wipe sweat from her brow.

'My, it's very hot in here,' Mallard said, playing along. 'Let's open the door to let the heat out.'

Old Man Winter jumped back from the door, afraid he might melt from the heat, and went back to his own lodge of ice and snow.

The next night Loon and Mallard worried that Old Man Winter would return. They knew his powers were strong. Would an icy wind snuff their fire out or blow away their wigwam? Would the pond be frozen solid, leaving them nothing to eat? That gave Loon an idea.

It is known that Old Man Winter has a weakness for certain winter foods. The nuts and dried red berries were already picked over by birds and squirrels. So Loon waded out into the cold marsh and gathered wild rice from the frozen, rust-coloured stalks. Then she decided to give a party and invite Old Man Winter to come.

No one but Spring can enter the frigid lodge of Winter and live. So Loon built up a hot fire in their own wigwam and began to cook the wild rice. Now and then she flapped her wings at the open door to send the sweet smell out into the world.

Before long, Old Man Winter came to Loon's door and asked sheepishly: 'Is that wild rice I smell in there? Shall I join you?'

Mallard served Old Man Winter a steaming bowl of rice with her good wing. Once again, icicles formed on the walls of the wigwam and snow swirled around them. While Old Man ate greedily,

Loon built the fire up to keep from shivering. She kept adding more and more wood to the fire.

Before long, the ice on Old Man Winter's face began to melt and he became smaller. He could feel himself shrink, but he didn't want to give up the delicious rice.

Suddenly Loon smiled and said: 'Spring must be here, Old Man, for my voice has returned.'

Old Man Winter, only the size of a bird himself, looked up with alarm. Now it was he who was voiceless. He ran from the wigwam and saw that all around him, flowers were blooming through patches of melting snow. His lodge of ice had caved into a muddy puddle.

That year Old Man Winter barely made his way back to the far North, hopping from snowpatch to snowpatch. Behind him he could hear the crazy laughter of a loon echoing through the forest.

Glossary

Cattail A reed plant found in marshy areas.

Cedar A large evergreen tree.

Kayak A one-man canoe made of a light wooden frame covered with sealskins.

Loon A diving bird that lives in large lakes, especially in Alaska and in the Great Lakes area of the USA.

Mesa A high, rocky, level surface with steep sides.

Moccasins Shoes or slippers made from deerskin or sheepskin.

Narwhal A type of whale with one large tusk.

Plains The wide, open grasslands at the heart of the North American continent.

Reservations Areas of land that belong to Native American communities.

Savannah A grassy, treeless plain in tropical regions.

Steppe A vast, grassy, treeless plain.

Tipi A conical tent made from an outer layer of skins on poles, traditionally used by Plains tribes.

Tribe A group of people or families living together under the rule of a chief.

Wigwam A tent or hut made out of wood and bark, traditionally used by Native Americans in the east of the USA.

Further Information

Storybooks:

The Best Tales Ever Told: Monsters and Magic, Myths and Legends from North and South America – Stewart Ross – Watts, 1998

Native North American Stories – retold by Robert Hull – Wayland, 1992

North American Myths and Legends – Philip Ardagh – Belitha Press, 1998

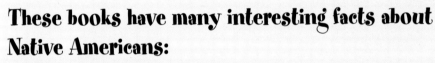

These books have many interesting facts about Native Americans:

Native Americans – Peoples Under Threat series – Helen L. Edmonds – Wayland, 1995

Native Americans – Threatened Cultures series – James Wilson – Wayland, 1992

What do we know about the Plains Indians? – Dr Colin Taylor – Macdonald Young Books, 1993

Website to visit:

A very good website to find more Native American myths, legends and traditional stories from different Native American tribes is at:

www.hanksville.org/storytellers/traditional

Native American Activities

In **The Ghost of the Ancient One**, many things make the main character shiver. Write your own ghost story based on what makes you shiver.

If you could turn into an animal as in **Manabozho and the Elk Skull**, what would you be? Write about your adventures and the new dangers you discover as your chosen animal. Remember to be somewhere safe when the spell wears off!

Write another chapter from Qasi's point of view beginning where **Qasi the Great Liar** ends.

The woman who was kept in the Water Monster's house in the **Navajo Creation Story** must have had an adventure of her own. Tell her account of what happened to her under the waves as she would have told her friends after she was rescued.

Compose a song or poem of **High Horse's Raid** that tells of High Horse's brave attempts to win the beautiful girl.

In **How Loon outsmarted Winter**, we learn all about Old Man Winter's harsh ways. Write about Loon's encounters with the other seasons. Think about how each season character might look and how they would act towards Loon.